THE POWER OF YOUR WORD

YEMI OYINKANSOLA

THE POWER OF YOUR WORD
Copyright © 2016 by **Yemi Oyinkansola**
ISBN: 978-1-944652-24-1

Printed in the United States of America. All rights reserved solely by the publisher. This book or parts thereof may not be reproduced in any form, stored in a retrieval system, or transmitted in any form by any means - electronic, mechanical, photocopy. Unless otherwise noted, Bible quotations are taken from the Holy Bible, New King James Version. Copyright 1982 by Thomas Nelson, Inc., publishers. Used by permission.

Published By:
Cornerstone Publishing
A division of Cornerstone Creativity Group LLC
Info@thecornerstonepublishers.com
www.thecornerstonepublishers.com

Author's Information
For speaking engagement or to order books
by Pastor Yemi Oyinkansola:
Info@yemioyinkansola.com | www.yemioyinkansola.com
+1 510.258.4583

CONTENTS

Dedication..7
Acknowledgment..8
Introduction..9

Chapter One
The Force In Your Word...13

Chapter Two
Nuggets From The Creation...21

Chapter Three
Your Tongue Is Your Life...29

Chapter Four
Speak Negative, See Negative......................................41

Chapter Five
Speak Life, See Life..53

Chapter Six
Thoughts And Words: The Connection.....................67

Chapter Seven
Confessing God's Words..................................83

Chapter Eight
The Power Of "I Can"..................................101

The Greatest Prayer Of A Lifetime........................113
About Pastor Yemi Oyinkansola............................114

DEDICATION

To all that love and believe the sure words of prophesy, the infallible word of God that is sharper than any two edged sword. There is power in the word of God.

ACKNOWLEDGMENT

I want to appreciate all my spiritual mentors for the positive impact their spoken word is having upon my life and ministry.

Thank you Cornerstone Publishing for completing this book in record time.

I acknowledge all my physical and spiritual family members and friends that have sharpen my life positively with their spoken words of encouragement and lifting.

I want to thank and appreciate my wife Comfort and my children Melody and Tolu for empowering me with their positive words whenever I'm tired and weary as a husband, father and Pastor. You guys are the best thing that has ever happened to me. Love you guys!

INTRODUCTION

Speech is one of the most defining characteristics of human beings. Statistics say that the average person spends one-fifth of his or her life talking. Through speech, we express our thoughts, convey our innermost desires and narrate our everyday encounters.

Beyond this, however, speech has also been confirmed to be a major determinant of the experiences of our lives and the directions of our destinies. Put simply, the words we speak have a great impact on our lives and what we eventually turn out to be. What you say and how you say it can either build your life or destroy it. It can either win you friends or enemies.

Sadly, it appears not many people understand this fundamental truth, judging by the way many speak so carelessly and negatively. Whether it's an angry mother talking to her child, a passenger who has just been outplayed by a taxi driver, colleagues having some conversations or individuals complaining about the challenges they are facing, the extent of negativity is so pervasive and quite disturbing.

I have equally discovered that, aside from the fact that many don't realize the power in their words, some people actually use unwholesome words because of the condition of their minds and the perception they have about themselves. They think small of themselves and don't see themselves achieving anything significant in life. In their own minds, they are failures or never-do-wells, probably because of recurring circumstances or what some other persons have said about them

While it is true that some persons don't mean some of the wrong things they say, nevertheless, they create negative realities for themselves because there is power in the spoken words. Words are so powerful that they can create, make alive, revive, and kill. This is why this book has been specially prepared – to show you how quickly things can turn around for you, depending on the things you think and say.

This is not just another book about positive speaking but about helping you take control of life by taking control of what you say. It is to help you see yourself in another light - to know that with the right perception and confession, you can achieve any goal you have set for yourself in accordance with God's purpose.

As you will discover through the eye-opening revelations, references and real life examples in this book, things aren't going to change until believers begin to change the way we think and speak. Our speech, thought pattern and what we think of ourselves must change if we want to experience any positive change in our circumstances.

This book will mark a turning point in your life. You will come to understand the power of the words you speak and make a decision to speak and think positively, thereby transforming your life and the life of those around you.

CHAPTER ONE

THE FORCE IN YOUR WORD

"Words are singularly the most powerful force available to humanity. We can choose to use this force constructively with words of encouragement, or destructively using words of despair." -Yehuda Berg

We live in a world where many seem to have little or no knowledge of the impact of the words they speak. To them, words are of little significance; they are just mere channels to convey their thoughts and feelings and nothing more. What they don't know, however, is that the words we speak actually end up as the cornerstones of our lives.

In the part of the world where I come from, I often

hear people say that what you don't know cannot harm you. Nothing can be further from the truth. What you don't know can actually kill you. If you don't know the effect the words you speak have over your life and the lives of others, you may have caused a lot of destruction before you know what's going on.

I have seen a lot of people experience defeat, failure, sickness, affliction, lack, fear and other unpleasant happenings because, having conceived such in their heart, they went on to confess them through their mouth. Though many times, these folks don't mean the negative things they say, unfortunately for them, these become the realities of their lives because there is power in the spoken words. As the quote from Yehuda Berg above shows, words are so powerful that they can create and make alive, just as they can weaken and kill.

The reality of this life is that both positive and negative experiences co-exist. While some people experience more of negative occurrences, some others have their lives full of the positive, beautiful, pleasant and glorious circumstances of life. The truth is that you decide on which part of the divide you want to belong or the kind of experience you want to be a daily part of your existence by the words you speak. You have a choice in life, by your confession, to choose which one to focus on so that it will eventually become part of your life. Positive or negative words spoken over your life can become your experience for the rest of your life. Whatever you speak over your life constantly will eventually become the real you.

PROOF OF IMPACT

There is this fable about a group of frogs which were traveling through the woods when, suddenly, two of them fell into a deep pit. All the other frogs gathered around the top of the pit wondering how their peers would ever get out. When they saw how deep the pit was, they told the unfortunate frogs that they would never get out. The two frogs ignored the comments of the other frogs and tried to jump up out of the pit. But each time they tried, they failed. The other frogs kept telling them to stop, that they were as good as dead. Finally, one of the frogs took heed to what the other frogs were saying and simply gave up trying to get out of the pit. He fell down and died. However, the other frog continued jumping as hard as he could. The more he tried, the more the crowd of frogs yelled at him to stop the pain and suffering and just die. But to their greatest surprise, he made one last hard and final jump and out he came!

When he got out, the other frogs asked him, "Why

did you continue jumping and struggling to come out? Didn't you hear us?" and to their greatest surprise again, they were shocked to know that the frog was deaf. All the time they were shouting at him, he actually thought they were all encouraging him to get out. He did not want to disappoint them and therefore did not give up till the end.

What this shows is the power of words and the impact they can have on people. While one frog died because it felt it was being discouraged by the words of the other frogs, the other survived because it felt motivated by the words of the other frogs. By implication, a negative and discouraging word sown into someone can kill such a person while a positive and encouraging word can lift a person and help him through the storm.

Your words have a great impact on your life and on others. Whether you are saying them jokingly or you mean them, the effects of your words can have a negative or a positive impact on you. That is why whether you are parent, pastor, boss or leader in whatever capacity, you must weigh the potential impact of your words before you let them out of our mouth.

The impact of your words can be damaging or building. Look at it this way, your word is a seed and every word you speak is a seed that is sown in the soil of life and in due time it will germinate. Every word you speak, be it positive or negative, has consequences.

In life, generally, it is the kind of seed you sow that will determine the kind of harvest you will have. You can't sow bitter-leaf and hope to reap sugarcane, and neither can you sow lemon and expect grapes when harvest time comes. It is a natural order or what some have referred to as the law of cause and effect. In the same vein, it is the kind of seeds you sow with your words that determine the kind of harvest or result you will have. Don't expect to speak negative words and get positive results. Things don't work that way.

YOUR LIFE IS A MIRROR OF YOUR WORDS

Just as a mirror reflects the image before it, your life reflects the words spoken to it. It is very much possible that your present state in life is a reflection of the words you have always believed and spoken consistently. If you've always believed that you can never do well in life and you say this often to yourself, even when things happen that are normal in life, you say they are happening because you're a failure, then you may never truly succeed. You are what you say. This is a basic fact.

There is this story of a blind boy who sat on the steps

of a building with a hat by his feet. He held up a sign which said: "I am blind, please help." Only a few people bothered to drop a few coins in the hat. After a while, a man walked towards the boy, took a few coins from his pocket and dropped them into the hat. He then took the sign, turned it around, and wrote some words. Then, he put the sign back so that everyone who walked by would see the new words.

It didn't take long before the hat began to fill up. A lot more people were giving money to the blind boy than before. Later that afternoon, the man who had changed the sign came to see how things were. The boy recognized his footsteps and asked, "Were you the one who changed my sign this morning.

"Yes," the man replied.

What did you write?" the blind boy asked again.

The man answered, "I only wrote the truth. I said what you said but in a different way. I wrote: "'Today is a beautiful day, but I cannot see it.'"

Can you see the power of words? Both signs basically said the same thing. They both told people that the boy was blind. But the difference was in the words used and the image the words conveyed. The first sign simply said the boy was blind; while the second sign reminded people how fortunate they were to have their sight. The second sign was more effective because the words were more positive. That's the power of words.

Additionally, a man's true personality can be gleaned from the words he speaks. As the philosopher, Publilius Syrus stated, "let a fool hold his tongue and he will pass for a sage." It is easy to conclude that a man is wise or otherwise through the way he speaks. This also means that our most definitive traits are easily betrayed or conveyed by the use of our mouth. What you say tells us who you are and what you're likely to become. It was William Shakespeare who once said that "Men of few words are the best men." This statement highlights the importance that is placed on the words that come out of our mouth and the impression they make about us.

Many people in their adult life reflect the words spoken over them by their parents when they were very young. It isn't unusual to find parents use abusive words on their children or even curse them outright in the heat of anger or disappointment. Sadly for some, it has even become a way of life and they see nothing wrong in it! Because these parents are ignorant of the power and impact of spoken words, they make it a way of life. In the long run, when the words they have so often spoken against their child begin to manifest in their child's life, they then begin to wonder where the problem is coming from. They caused it. They cursed their children.

You remember the story of Jabez in 1 Chronicles 4:9-10. The Scripture records that because of the pain and suffering his mother went through within the period of his birth, she named him "Sorrow" - and that was all that was needed to make the life of this young man miserable. The word "sorrow" became his identity and his reality. From family members to friends, neighbors and strangers, everyone called him Sorrow. And as long as he was under the influence of that word, he never succeeded. Things would have continued to go downward for Jabez if he hadn't decided to challenge the influence of that word over his life in prayer. But how many years of his life had been wasted by the carelessness of his mother!

Be careful of what you say then. Don't underestimate the power of words. There is no telling to what extent that little word of yours may go, how far the good it can do or how damaging the harm it can cause. But why do words have so much power and impact on our lives? Well, it's the way God has designed the world to function from the very beginning. Let's go on to see proof of this!

CHAPTER TWO

NUGGETS FROM THE CREATION

"In the beginning God created the heaven and the earth. And the earth was without form, and void; and darkness was upon the face of the deep. And the Spirit of God moved upon the face of the waters. And God said, Let there be light: and there was light." - Genesis 1:1-3

The first book of the Bible gives us a vivid description of how God created the world and provides deep insight into the power of the spoken word. We read in Genesis that God, the Self-existing, Almighty and All-knowing One, spoke the universe into existence. On six consecutive days, God spoke out what He wanted to see take place on the earth. He spoke out His desires and they became reality.

The expression "God said" occurs seven times before the creation of man. That aside, before God started to speak, the earth had been void, dark and formless. It was all silent and gloomy, until God began to speak. God wasn't perturbed. He didn't become worried or discouraged because of the state of the earth at that time. He knew there was creative power in His words.

What this confirms to us, therefore, is that God didn't create the earth by using any process of evolution. The creation of the earth was solely engineered and brought about by the creative ability of His word. It wasn't by chance or circumstances, but by a deliberate act of speaking.

Additionally, we discover that there seems to be a relationship between the will of God and the words of God. God had an idea of what He wanted the earth to look like. In a manner of speaking, He could see the whole picture in His mind. He willed it. He wanted it. But to bring it into reality, He had to give it expression; he had to speak it out.

So, in essence, every time God spoke, the words were bringing forth what was in His mind; for speaking is a revelation of thought. The words were bringing forth the will of God. They happened because God desired them and spoke them out. It means, therefore, that if God had only pictured them in His mind without speaking them forth, they wouldn't have happened. It is not enough to desire something; that desire must be expressed!

Another thing we discover is the correlation between what is seen and what is said. Notice in Genesis 1, that every time there is a "God said", it is always ends with "and God saw." Whenever God spoke anything He wanted to be done, he saw it happen. God couldn't see anything, unless and until He said it. This means that there is a definite connection between confession and manifestation; a cause and effect relationship.

Whatever happens is as a result of what has been said. What is said is the causative while what is seen is the effect. Nothing happens until it is said, and whatever is said happens whether it be good or bad. Nothing in the creation happened by chance. God saw that everything he made was good because everything he said was positive.

From the foregoing, it is now abundantly clear, that everything in existence today came out of the power of the words spoken by the mouth of God the Creator Himself. They exist because God spoke them. This much is confirmed in Hebrews 11:3, where the Scriptures say that **"through faith we understand that the worlds were framed by the word of God, so that things which are seen were not made of things which do appear."** What we discover, therefore, is that creative ability resides in God's spoken word.

So, without any fear of contradiction, we can say that the Almighty God is a speaking God. Aside from the fact that He spoke the earth into being, it is still existing today because He is holding everything together by His powerful word (Hebrews 1:3). This means that God is still speaking today and His word is still havin impact on the world.

CREATED IN HIS IMAGE

From the Bible, we understand that of all the creations of God, man was the only one that wasn't spoken into existence. Adam, the first man, was created—formed from the dust of the ground—in the image of God (Genesis 1:26-27). What this means, in essence, is that unlike other things that God created, man was created to have unique capabilities just like God. He was created to be God-like in appearance, attitude and existence. He was created with inherent abilities to talk, act and live like God.

The reason for this is because of the peculiarity and importance of man in God's plan for the world. Interestingly, it is evident that God gave the same creative power of the spoken word to Adam. Since he was created in the image of God, it only follows that his words should carry in them the ability to create reality. It isn't only logical, it is also scripturally true.

So, Adam received from God, the creative possibilities inherent in words. Evidence of this can be seen in God's fellowship and relationship with him. God placed man on earth to be its king and to rule over everything in it. What God was in heaven, man was to be on earth. Whatever he said became law therein. We can glean this from the occasion when Adam gave names to all the creatures of God. Whatever Adam uttered became the original name of every animal or creature till today (Genesis 2:19).

God entrusted Adam with this task because he possessed the wisdom of God. More so, you will remember that Adam also named Eve, the woman God created and brought to him to be his wife. He demonstrated authority and used his mouth rightly by speaking positively and God saw that everything that had manifested up until that point was good.

THE WRONG TURN

Evidently, everything the man had spoken with his mouth from the time of his creation to the naming of Eve was only positive. This was possible because of his sinless state. Regrettably, everything took a wrong turn when the serpent came speaking dangerous words and the couple listened.

God had given the man everything in the Garden for food in Genesis 2:16-17. But he was expressly forbidden to eat from the tree of the knowledge of good and evil. He and his wife obviously obeyed this directive until the devil came into the garden, turning their hearts away from God by the words he spoke.

Eve was deceived by the devil's words. She listened to his words and allowed him to sow the seed of his lies in the soil of her mind; it germinated and the manifestation was disobedience against God. But it didn't end there. Maybe if it had, the human race would have been saved from its present predicaments.

When Adam returned from wherever he might have gone, I could picture Eve speaking to her husband about what the devil had said and how she had gone on to test it and how her eyes had been enlightened. With her many fair words, she convinced him to eat the forbidden fruit and he did it. Unfortunately for them both, by this action, they fell from grace to grass, from innocence to judgment.

Perhaps, the situation could still have been remedied if only one of them had used her lips wisely. The catastrophe that followed could probably have been avoided if they had only spoken the right words. But they didn't.

When God walked into the garden in the cool of the day to fellowship with the man and his wife, as he had always done, the couple had gone into hiding. Of course, God knew what they had done, but he would have willingly forgiven them if only they had taken the right approach by confessing with their mouth. Regrettably, the words they spoke cost them their relationship with God and settled their destiny. They were driven out of the beautiful garden to labor on a cursed ground.

SO SHALL IT ALWAYS BE

But couldn't this calamity have been avoided? Yes, it could, if only the right words had been spoken. Notice that it all started with spoken words and got worse by spoken words. The devil used his words to deceive the woman into disobeying God; the woman, in turn, used her words to entice the man and convinced him to turn away from obeying God's word. When the time of reckoning came, the man turned around to blame God for giving him a wife he didn't ask for in the first place!

It is obvious therefore that the power inherent in the words we speak didn't just begin today. It has always been so right from the beginning of time. Things have not changed. The words we speak have not lost their power or force. As long as we remain on the surface of the earth, the things we say will continue to have an effect on the things we see; they will continue to create reality; for that was the way it was at the beginning and so shall it always be.

CHAPTER THREE

YOUR TONGUE IS YOUR LIFE

We have seen that the words we speak have the power to create a positive or negative reality. This, therefore, means that your tongue plays a very critical function in determining what your life eventually becomes. In other words, your tongue is your life, for whatever it utters defines you.

In the light of this, I shall be exploring this theme further in this chapter. In doing this, I will look first at the description of the tongue, the little member inside the mouth that is actually used in articulating the words we speak. This is necessary because in many cases, the tongue is actually used to refer to the mouth; and in this book, when I talk about the tongue, I'm actually referring to the mouth. Both words will subsequently be used interchangeably.

WHAT IS THE HUMAN TONGUE?

Oxford Advanced Learner's Dictionary defines the tongue as, 'the soft part in the mouth that moves around, used for tasting, swallowing, speaking , etc.' It is also described as the fleshy muscular organ in the mouth of a mammal, used for tasting, licking, swallowing, and (in humans) articulating speech. Dictionary.com defines the tongue as "the usually movable organ in the floor of the mouth of humans and most vertebrates, functioning in eating, in tasting, and in humans, in speaking.

Now, although in these definitions, 'speaking' and 'articulating speech' occupy the last positions in the list of the functions the human tongue performs, the use of the tongue for communication is the most important and destiny-defining function of the tongue. In this last function, interpersonal relationships are enhanced, inspiration or fear can be created, war or peace can be incited, homes are built or destroyed, and so on. In fact, there is no evil or good that occurs without the tongue. Let's now turn to the word of God for its own description of the tongue.

WHAT DOES THE BIBLE SAY ABOUT THE TONGUE?

If you do a close reading of the Holy Bible, you will discover that, in its comprehensiveness, it deploys some terrific but accurate metaphors in describing the power and potency of the human tongue. The Bible compares the tongue to a fire, a burning fire in James 3:5 and Proverbs 16:27. In James 3:6-8, it compares the tongue to a world of iniquity, a beast that needs taming and then as a fountain of either fresh or bitter water later in verse 11. More so, it goes on to say that the tongue is a tree bearing either good or evil fruit (James 3:12), an unruly evil (James 3:8), deadly poison (James 3:8), a sharp razor, a sharp sword (Psalms 52:2; 57:4; 59:7), a poisonous serpent (Psalms 140:3), a deep pit (Proverbs 22:14), etc.

The inherent juxtaposition in the metaphorical representation of the tongue in the Holy Writ clearly portrays the tongue as a source of both good and evil, sweetness and bitterness, and life and death. It is also clear from the foregoing that unguarded and unguided use of the tongue is prone to doing more evil than good. Thus, the Bible paints it as 'a deep pit,' 'a sharp razor,' 'deadly poison,' 'a beast,' 'an unruly evil,' 'a sharp sword,' 'a world of iniquity,' and ' a poisonous serpent.'

DEATH AND LIFE IN THE TONGUE

When the Scriptures say in Proverbs 18:21 that **"Death and life are in the power of the tongue,"** it is saying unequivocally, that the tongue simultaneously possesses the power to evoke both good and bad fortunes in the life of any man. The power to cause the greatest good and the power to inflict or trigger the worst evil are housed in the tongue.

A man may become blessed or cursed simply because of the way he uses his tongue. Matthew Henry highlights this point when he says that, "A man may do a great deal of good, or a great deal of hurt, both to others and to himself, according to the use he makes of his tongue. Many a one has been his own death by a foul tongue, or the death of others by a false tongue; and, on the contrary, many a one has saved his own life, or procured the comfort of it, by a prudent gentle tongue."

We all have the choice to either use our tongue positively or negatively. Yes, you do have a choice to either use your tongue for good or use it for evil. So, to whichever function you choose to employ your tongue, you will eat or bear the consequences of the fruit it bears, either good or bad, sweet or bitter, positive or negative, glorious or shameful. The choice is yours.

It is also worthy of note that men who ever became truly great, both in Bible days and in contemporary times, were men who were blessed by a positively used tongue; and correspondingly, the man through whom the tongue has been used wrongly goes out of favor with men and God.

From the Scriptures, we find that through the use of the tongue, some were pronounced blessed while others were cursed. They were made either victors or victims by the use of their tongue. The difference between Abraham, Isaac, Jacob on the one hand and Cain and Reuben on the other hand, lies in the fact that the former set of people were blessed, while the latter set was cursed.

All Abraham needed to become the father of all nations was not a huge capital base for an investment in an oil business; he only needed God to pronounce him blessed. Had God blessed Cain after the killing of Abel, he would, as well, have succeeded in life. In the same vein, the greatness of Jacob can be traced to the fact that he got his father's blessings before his elder brother, Esau. Esau knew that his glory and all that he would ever become was tied to the blessings that proceeded from the mouth of his father. This was why he wept sore on realizing that his brother had received the blessings in his stead.

Even their father, Isaac, was not ignorant of the power in his mouth. He knew that as a father, his words would wield enormous influence over his children's destinies. He knew that whatever came out of his mouth would surely take effect. Therefore, he did not take his utterances for granted. The carefulness he showed in an attempt to avoid giving the blessing to the wrong person shows he knew that his mouth could make a lord out of whoever receives the blessing. This is why Esau's belated return for the blessing was greeted with such finality: **"Behold, I have made [Jacob] thy lord [by my words]"** (Genesis 27: 37). This accentuates the power of the tongue as well as the irretrievability of spoken words.

CONFESSION AND POSSESSION

The distance a man can go in life is not solely dependent on what is conceived in the mind, but also by what he speaks with his mouth. Thoughts are conceived in the mind and activated by the tongue. The limit of your success is set by the tongue, so also is the foundation of your failure.

The Promise Land was willed to the children of Israel by an act of divine benevolence. Unfortunately, not all of them eventually got there. What became the ticket of entrance for Caleb and Joshua was the same thing that denied the other ten spies entrance into the Promised Land – their tongue. Twelve of them went to spy the land; they all observed that the land was rich, lush and fertile. They even brought samples of fruits from there as a testament to their report and they all saw the children of Anak. However, the contrast was in the reports they gave with their mouths. It was this that set them apart and defined their destinies.

The Bible's record of God's response to them is very instructive. God said, **"Say unto them, As truly as I live, saith the Lord, as ye have spoken in mine ears, so will I do to you"** (Numbers 14: 28). As an Arabian adage goes, "when you have spoken the word, it reigns over you; when it is unspoken you reign over it," those who said they were not able to possess the land all perished in the wilderness but Caleb and Joshua secured for themselves the Promised Land as well as an eternity of fame through the use of their mouth.

God respects the power of the tongue. What you say concerning yourself becomes like a constitution in the hands of God with which He performs certain operations in your life. This is why it is not wise to speak foolishly and negatively about yourself. Negative confessions about yourself hinder God on the issues of your life.

Jesus, underscoring the importance of the tongue, declared to Peter and the other disciples and by extension, all the children of God thus: **"And I will give unto thee the keys of the kingdom of heaven: and whatsoever thou shalt bind on earth shall be bound in heaven: and whatsoever thou shalt loose on earth shall be loosed in heaven"** (Matt 16:19; 18:18). Jesus could have said, "whatsoever you wish to bind on earth shall be bound in heaven: and whatsoever you wish to loose on earth shall be loosed in heaven" but that would have rendered the potency of the tongue useless and irrelevant. It, then, goes without saying that what you become or what becomes of you depends more on what you say than what you wish.

More so, in our dealings with men and professions to ourselves, the devil takes inventory of what we say. He uses them as evidence against us before God when he goes on his accusation mission. Supposing you keep telling yourself or people around you that you can't be anything good in this life. Even if God is willing to make you something great, the devil will withstand him with the same words you spoke as the reason why God must not help you. This can make the hands of God tight in the situation of a man.

While unbelief is not in any way encouraged, it is better to keep quiet even when we do not believe than to utter our unbelief. In the same vein, if you have nothing good to say about yourself or about a situation it is better to stay quiet and say nothing at all. There is an incidence in the Bible that perfectly underscores this point. In the seventh verse of second kings, a great famine had spread Samaria.

The gravity of the famine had been catastrophic and unprecedented. But in the midst of this, came Elisha the prophet who prophesied that notwithstanding the great tragedy in the city, there would plenty to eat within twenty-four hours from the time of his prophecy. The prophecy itself was as odd as it was unexpected. How could Elisha have prophesied that? Didn't he know the amount of hunger, deprivation and suffering in the land to have made such a radical pronouncement? Of course, he knew. But he was speaking as an oracle of God and where the word of God is, there is power. "Man's extremity is God's opportunity of magnifying his own power; his time to appear for his people is when their strength is gone" (Matthew Henry).

Now, there was a courtier for whom the king had affection and on whom he reposed much confidence. This man doubted the proclamation of hope and plenty. Probably a lot of other people doubted too. But they were wise to keep their mouth shut. But this man didn't. He spoke too soon and too rashly. He thought it impossible for God to turn Samaria's woes around in one day, except there was a miracle like in the days of Moses when God rained manna from Heaven. Unfortunately for this man, the miracle did happen, God did turn around the situation within a day, but he didn't partake in the miracle. His mouth killed him (2 Kings 7:1-29).

The circumstances surrounding the man's response to Elisha is justifiable from a human point of view. It was a period of severe famine and extreme dearth. Women became cannibals just to assuage the rage of hunger in the land. The king was in a perpetual state of mourning. There was no food to eat. People even bought dove's dung to eat. It was a pathetic situation. So, it can be argued that he had a reason to disbelieve the prophet. It is also glaring that unbelief itself was not the cause of his death; the cause of his death was his tongue. I want to believe that there were many others who did not believe the prophet considering the situation of the land and the sudden surplus that he prophesied but none of them died because they kept quiet and held their unbelief in silence.

You don't have to join the train of pessimists and

cynics no matter what you are passing through. Pessimism and negative confessions can entangle you and make you lose the battles of your life as the Bible puts it, **"Thou art snared with the words of thy mouth; thou art taken with the words of thy mouth."** (Proverbs 6:2) Positive confession possesses the ability to set you free. When the chips are down, always learn to say, "It is well" and everything will be well. Stay positive; speak positively!

CHAPTER FOUR

SPEAK NEGATIVE, SEE NEGATIVE

I have already established the fact that although the tongue appears to be a little member of the body, it can greatly define a man's life. It is a very great instrument that can either build or destroy. It can set a whole forest on fire from just a small spark. Regrettably, because many people do not realize the power of the tongue, the words that we speak, and the impact that they make on our lives and the lives of those around us, they use their mouth negatively.

The Scripture tells us in Proverbs 18:21 "Death and life are in the power of the tongue: and they that love it shall eat the fruit thereof." In the same vein, you will eat what you speak; the outcome of your future is a product of what you speak, whether good or bad. The earlier we realize this, the better it will save us from some avoidable problems.

There is no doubt that the misuse of the tongue cuts across all races, religions, tribes and communities. Parents have used it to either build or destroy the lives of their children. Some religious leaders have used it to bless or curse their followers. Politicians have often applied it maliciously against one another. Employees have also used it to mar the careers of their superiors, subordinates or themselves. No doubt, its careless use has promoted hatred, increased and spread lies, broken relationships, torn families and has been the cause of conflicts and wars.

Nowadays, almost everywhere you go, it's more common to find people who use their mouths negatively than it is to find those who speak positively. Why do people misuse their tongues? The reasons aren't farfetched: hatred, bias, uncontrolled anger, pride, selfishness, ignorance, and such likes.

How do people use their tongues negatively?

1. Gossip

"I am more deadly than the screaming shell of the

canon. I win without killing, I tear down homes, break hearts, wreck lives. I travel on the wings of the wind. No innocent is strong enough to intimidate me, no purity strong enough to daunt me. I have no regard for truth, no respect for justice, no mercy for the defenseless. My victims are so numerous as the sands of the sea and often as innocent. I never forget and seldom forgive. My name is GOSSIP" (extracted from Grady Scott's "BE CAREFUL LITTLE TONGUE WHAT YOU SAY").

Gossip is an idle talk or rumor, especially about the personal or private affairs of others. It is widely known and seen amongst people, unfortunately, it has crept into Christian circles today. People gossip about just anybody and everybody: neighbors, friends and even religious leaders. To some people, it has even become a trade or occupation and we see numerous examples of this on the social media. People spread rumors about others without feeling any restraint within them. They conveniently tarnish the image of people without verifying the truth. What baffles one is how they expect to succeed in life by deliberately running others down. God frowns at this.

2. Murmuring and Complaining

This is a low or indistinct continuous sound, a quiet

expression of an opinion or feeling, speech or a way of speaking that is quiet and soft. It is also a form of complaining that harbors a negative attitude towards a situation or the people involved. When you are told about something and you have to disagree with it, do you show your displeasure in a good way or you murmur to find your way through?

The Scripture strictly warns against murmuring in I Corinthians 10:10: **"Neither murmur ye, as some of them also murmured and were destroyed of the destroyer..."** and Philippians 2:14-15: **"Do all things without murmuring..."** Murmuring ignores God's promises and it's always born in the context of bad report. The tongue, if misused, can create an environment in which murmuring can thrive. Some people are eager to hear negative things so they can have something to complain about. A murmuring spirit is quick to jump to the wrong conclusion. The grumbling Israelites blamed God for their situation and even began planning to return to Egypt. When godless grumbling begins to spread, wrong conclusions are easily reached.

Murmuring leads to self-pity; murmurers often feel sorry for themselves and focus on how they have been mistreated, misused and let down. Murmurers find it difficult to manifest faith because murmuring thrives in an atmosphere of fear and the end result of a murmuring spirit is a general atmosphere of dissatisfaction. Murmuring does nothing but cause unneeded stress, deteriorates your faith, gives Satan an opportunity to sneak into your life and gives you a poor testimony.

I used to think that people complain because they have problems but now I know and realize that many have problems because they complain. An attitude of grumbling, griping, murmuring or squawking doesn't change anything and neither does it make situations better. It only amplifies frustration, expresses unbelief, spread discontent among others. No matter what you are going through, no matter the circumstances on your way, murmuring and complaining isn't the solution to any problem or challenge.

If anyone ever had the room to complain about his circumstances, it would be Paul who suffered greatly for the cause of Christ and wrote much of the Pauline epistles from a prison cell. He recounted his experience in 2 Corinthians 11:24-28, but despite all, Paul didn't surrender to a bitter or complaining attitude but kept his focus on the bright side of life (Philippians 4:11). If one keeps a good attitude and remains steadfast in faith, God will even turn seemingly ugly situations around and work them all out together for good. Don't become bitter and resort to complaining but speak positively and continue to praise God in spite of all things. Let's avoid a negative lifestyle of complaining and put on the attitude of praise.

3. Making rash vows

Most people find themselves in this situation because of pressure to meet certain urgent needs. They make vows that they know quite that they cannot fulfill. They make rash decisions even without thinking and the end result is always disastrous.

The story of Jephthah (Judges 11) illustrates the foolishness of using the mouth wrongly in making vows without understanding the consequences. Before leading the Israelites into battle against the Ammonites, Jephthah - described as a mighty man of valor - made a rash vow that he would give to the lord whoever first came out of the door to meet him if he returned home as the victor. The Lord granted him victory. Unfortunately, however, the one who came out to meet him was his daughter. You can imagine the look of horror on his face when he saw her.

Also, in Joshua 9, the Israelites made a covenant with the Gibeonites, who came under the false pretense that they lived far away and wanted to make peace with Israel since they heard that their God was going to wipe out any of the people of the land. Once the Israelites made the vow, they were compelled to honor it, although it was not according to God's desire.

King Saul made a similarly rash vow in 1 Samuel 14 when he commanded that if any of his soldiers ate during a battle, they would be put to death (cursed). His son, Jonathan, wasn't present when the vow was made; so, when he found honey in the wood, he ate some. In this case, however, Saul's soldiers convinced him not to keep the vow because it was rash and harsh.

King Herod also made a promise to his step-daughter that he would give her anything, up to half of his kingdom. That careless vow led to the beheading of John the Baptist. Proverbs 6 says that if you make a rash promise that you later regret, you must approach the person and ask for a release from the promise, if they do not grant it, then you are obligated. The difficulty comes when the thing you agreed to would violate some other moral principles, especially if what it would violate is much more important than keeping your word, like the case of Jephthah.

4. Lying

Lying is a huge issue for many people, including supposed Christians. It is one of the most common forms of negative speaking. "A lie is a false statement made with deliberate intent to deceive…" (Random House College Dictionary). In Acts 5:1-9, Ananias and his wife, Sapphira, sold their property and gave part of the money to the church, but they lied that they gave the whole money for the property sold.

Often, because people want to make a favorable impression on others, they say nice things that they don't really mean or don't really believe to be true. This may seem kind but it is a form of deliberately deceiving others. In Psalm 62:4, the Bible describes such as those who **"delight in lies: they bless with their mouth, but they curse inwardly."** When we don't mean the nice things we say, we are lying. This may remind us of politicians trying to get votes; they pretend to think highly of you but they only want something from you.

Sometimes we really hold an unfavorable view of someone, but we don't want to insult them, so it is easy to say what we don't mean. Perhaps it isn't even proper for us to be thinking negative thoughts about others, but if our thoughts are valid, then we either speak the truth or find something we can honestly say or just change the subject, but lying should not be an option.

Some people think they are innocent as long as they

say what is technically true even though they intent to mislead others to believe what is not true. It is possible to tell things that are technically true, yet we leave out pertinent facts or otherwise so that we lead others to believe untruths.

We are not required to tell people everything we know; some things are confidential or there may be no good reason why some particular persons should be told certain things but lying isn't the way to go; it's a negative use of the tongue.

Anyone who lies belongs to Satan because we are told in the Scripture that he is the father of all liars (John 8:4). Satan influences men to lie. Often, businesses tell lies to convince people to buy their products; some companies even require employees to lie. And then there are some people who cover up evil deeds with lies like Gehazi, Elisha's servant, who lied to cover up his deeds (2 Kings 5:20-27). People no longer trust one another because many have taught their mouths to lie.

Lies can result in hatred as we see in the case of Jacob and his sons. It could also lead to strife and alienation for the rest of one's life. Many of us know families in which people have been alienated from one another because of lies. One of the main lessons to be learnt from Jacob's family is the severe problems that deceit can cause. If you want a good family life, one thing you need to develop in a relationship is trust and honesty.

Lying often destroys people's reputations or alienate people, not only in families but also at workplaces, at school and in church. When people find out that others have lied to them or about them, they are often hurt and angry. Lying leads to loss of respect and confidence.

5. Cursing

Curse is an appeal or prayer for evil or misfortune to befall someone or something. Your speech reveals what is going on inside you. Using foul language indicates that you are insensitive to the feelings of others. Cursing can cause others to think negatively of you. The way we speak can determine who our friends will be, the amount of respect we get from our family and co-workers, the quality of our relationship, the level of our influence, whether we get the job or the promotion, and how strangers respond to us.

In the book How Rude, Dr. Alex Packer States: "people who swear (curse) all the time are tiresome to listen to. If your speech is lazy, vague and imaginative, your mind is sure to follow. God says cursing and filthy language is wrong because it lowers his Holy name to the level of sinful man, it also lowers the beautiful relationship between a husband and wife to the level of animals, it also destroys the sacredness of the human body."

NEGATIVE SPEAKING GENERATES NEGATIVE EXPERIENCES

Our sub-conscious mind works on pure logic and does not know about context when we use language. Unless we pay particular conscious attention to context, the subconscious will often pick out key words in a sentence and use those to generate experience or feelings. If most of the words are negatives or have negative associations for our subconscious, then most of the experiences and feelings will tend towards the negatives.

Avoid speaking or saying negative things or surrounding yourself with people who speak negatively. God says he has plans to prosper you, not to harm you; so avoid saying things like "I'm broke", "I have no money and I'm barely making it." These go against the blessings God has in store for you. Instead, say "I'm wealthy", "I have more than enough," "My God shall supply all my needs."

The next time you want to say "No one loves me," go

to John 15:9 and be reminded of how God loves you. If you're in debt, instead of saying I'll never get out of debt, read Deuteronomy 28:12, where God says you will lend to many nations and you will not borrow. As Christians, we need to stop blocking God's blessings by speaking negatively. God wants to bless us but we become a hindrance in receiving his blessings. The very essence of our being was spoken into existence by God. So, monitor what you speak.

Be reminded again that words are powerful; they are seeds that yield a good or bad harvest (depending on what you speak). There is power in finding scriptures on your particular situation and speaking what God has to say about it instead of what your flesh or others say about it. God wants to bless you; don't let your mouth stay in the way of your blessings. We'll talk more about these in subsequent chapters.

Let this chapter end every negative speaking in your life. You can be positive.

CHAPTER FIVE

SPEAK LIFE, SEE LIFE

In chapter four, we took a look at numerous ways in which people use their tongues wrongly and negatively. Many of those actively engaged in this activity are oblivious of the effect and influence of their words on their own lives and that of others.

In contrast, there are those who understand that the words they speak have a direct influence on their lives and therefore put their mouths to positive use and prospered from it. There are Christians who feel that it's only when things are rosy that they can only speak positively. This shouldn't be so. Using your mouth positively should be the lifestyle of a Christian.

In the next chapter, we'll look at the power of positive

confession. But here, let me briefly share four inspiring stories of people who have used their mouth positively and the huge benefits it accrued to their life. These are no fictions at all; they are real life stories of real people, both in the Bible times and in our contemporary days. If these people could use their mouth positively when things looked gloomy and hopeless, you also can make speaking positively a personal habit in order to experience the supernatural.

WE ARE ABLE

In Numbers 13, we read of how God instructed Moses to send twelve men to search the land of Canaan (which was promised to them as an inheritance). After spending forty days on the trip, these spies returned with clusters of grapes, pomegranates and figs which attested to the fact that the land was indeed flowing with milk and honey.

Nevertheless, ten of the spies spoke words of fear and defeat into the hearts of the people. These ten men used their mouths negatively. If they had stopped at describing what they saw in the land, it would have been good but they went further to underestimate the power of the God of Israel - the God who parted the Red Sea before them when all hope was lost and destroyed all their enemies with their chariots of horses. They rubbished the might and authority of God in the eyes of the people by emphatically stating that they cannot conquer the land because the people there were stronger than Israel.

Maybe this was true; maybe the citizens of Canaan were indeed physically stronger than Israel. But since God had promised to give them the land, they should never have contradicted that with their words. They made God a liar and incited the people to lose their faith in God because they spoke words of fear and defeat.

But Caleb and Joshua were wise enough to use their tongues positively. They believed that they could possess the land according to the word of God. They were in the minority but stood by their faith and conviction. They even tried to comfort the hearts of the people and encouraged them to stay positive but the people refused to listen to them. Incited by the words of the ten spies, they blasphemed against God and voiced out that it would have been better if God had killed them in Egypt or in the wilderness. And true to their words, they all perished in the wilderness according to the words of their mouth while Caleb and Joshua were the only ones who made it to Canaan.

The only difference between Caleb and Joshua and the rest was the positive words they confessed. God takes our words into account. If the very hairs of our head are all numbered, how much more the words that proceed from our mouth!

"Say unto them, as truly as I live saith the Lord, as ye have spoken in my ears so will I do to you" (Numbers 14:28). This was God speaking to the children of Israel and that word is still applicable to you today. Every single thing you say will come to pass.

A FATHER'S UNWAVERING CONFESSIONS

There is a remarkable and compelling story of a father, Norvel and his daughter, Zona. Norvel's experience illustrates how powerful our utterances can be even when things are not seemingly okay.

Just like every average person will act on impulse rather than on the written word of God, Norvel, though a Pastor, used to respond to situations based on his feelings but God taught him to confess the words of faith even when every hope seems gone. And not until he began to confess positively with a reckless abandon did he begin to see the changes he wanted.

Norvel's wife left him when their daughter was nine. It was a devastating experience for the father and daughter but they had to carry on. In her late teenage years, Zona began dating a guy named Bobby who was also a member of their church. They both loved God and continued to pursue their career. They planned to get married when Bobby got out of service while Zona would, by then, be in her second year in college. However, after some time, God told Norvel that He didn't want his daughter to marry Bobby. He also counseled him to watch the boy closely. Sadly, he couldn't convince her to cancel the marriage and they got married eventually. But after a year, they were divorced.

Things began to go from bad to worse as Zona began to live recklessly. She stopped going to church and as a minister's child, it hurt her dad so much to see his daughter living below moral and spiritual standards. For three and half years, she was immersed in drugs, partying and other vices. She deteriorated to the point that she took up to twelve pills per day.

Initially, Norvel's responses towards his daughter were based on how he felt—negative. Norvel would constantly tell her that she was a disgrace to the family, that she was a big disappointment. There was even a time when he told her that he wished she were dead.

He said he would rather lose her than go through all the agony she was causing him, but this only drew her farther and farther from God. She came to believe that nobody loved her, not even God. She did not cease to sneer at him by saying "how does it make you feel to know that you can go and win all other kids to the Lord and you can't even do anything for your own child?"

After Norvel had prayed for two years without results, God finally told him a hard truth. God told him that until his faith was unwavering and he showed his daughter genuine love like He showed to him when he was still in sin, He would not grant his request. Isn't it strange and ironical how some people pray about something and confess the opposite? God knows when our words and actions match our prayers. God sees through the veil and He can tell the state of our hearts. When we pray to God as a sign of formality and we confess negatively afterward, we'll beget negative results.

From that day, Norvel never said anything negative about his daughter anymore. When she returned home at 1 a.m., he would have her sit beside him and tell her how much he loved her. In his words, "Every time Zona would put on her mini skirt and walk out the door, I would go to the picture window. As I looked out, I would stand on God's word, quoting His promises. As I watched her drive off, I would tell the devil, I won't let you have her. You're not going to kill her. I would say, thank you, Jesus, for bringing Zona back to the Kingdom. I just kept on thanking God that Zona was coming back to the family of God". Even when there weren't obvious results, he kept on confessing positively about his daughter and thanking God for the answers.

Miraculously, Zona's life was transformed through the positive attitude and confession of her father. Her marriage was restored and her husband rededicated his life to God. Both of them are doing great things for God today, though most of her friends have died because of drugs. She strongly believes that her father's unwavering confessions of faith over her life are the only reason she is still alive today. Together, Zona and her father authored Stand in the Gap for your Children, a book which has touched many lives.

YOU AREN'T WANTED HERE IF YOU CAN'T SPEAK POSITIVELY

Oral Roberts' mother was a woman who did not tolerate negative confessions about her family from anyone, not even the devil. As an Indian who married a white man when racial discrimination was prevalent, she displayed a great deal of strength and courage.

When Oral was born, he was a stutterer and he felt so different from other kids. His mother, however, continued to confess positively into his life because she knew about God's promises. Back then, Medical science witnessed so much breakthrough and there weren't cure for a lot of diseases, but she would either say, "Oral, your body is frail, but no matter what happens, you're going to make it" or "Oral, God is going to heal your stuttering and you will talk" or "Here, read these books, learn all you can. Remember all you learn, and never settle for anything but your best". And true to her words, God healed him of stuttering.

There is this particularly inspiring story that I read about Oral's mother. There was a time Oral became ill with tuberculosis and there was no cure for it. She had seen people die of TB in the past but she confessed and believed her son would live. Because the disease had no cure, a lot of church people visited their home and said all manner of things to Oral. Some believed God put the disease on him to teach him a lesson while others said that it might not be God's will to heal him.

His mother rose to action one day and told them point

blank that although she appreciated their visit, if they believed that God had put TB on her son and may not heal him, then, they should leave their house and never come back until they could lift his faith by their words and not tear it down.

Here is positivity in action. That mother knew the power of spoken words and wouldn't permit negative words to be spoken over her sick child. She was simply saying, "If you can't speak positively about my son's sickness, then you aren't wanted anywhere near him. Don't destroy his life with your negative words."

When I read this part in Oral's autobiography, I trembled at the awesome revelation his mother had about faith and positive confession in that age and time. In the long run, it so happened that he was not only healed of stuttering and tuberculosis, he became one of the famous religious figures of the twentieth century until he died at 91.

THE WISE WOMAN WHO PRESERVED HER HOUSEHOLD

The story of Abigail (1 Samuel 25) is worth remembering over and over again. She didn't have the weapons of war or the skill to fight a battle but she used her mouth to avert a conflict which would have wiped out her entire household. The destruction that should have been unleashed on her family was as a result of her husband's brutish, callous and churlish attitude towards David and the misuse of his mouth.

At this time, David was still a fugitive who was fleeing from place to place in order to escape from Saul. Nabal, Abigail's husband was a very rich man whose shepherds were protected by David in the wilderness. David heard the news that Nabal was shearing his sheep and he sent his men to seek his favor in the most respectable way.

Ordinarily, one would think that these words would soften the heart of Nabal and he would be kind enough to give David something to sustain himself and his team in the wilderness. Of course, Nabal could afford to be kind because he was a very rich man; more so, David had been used by God to protect his shepherds in the wilderness. Shockingly, what David got in response was outrage and disgust from Nabal. In fact, he asked, "Who is this David? And who is the son of Jesse?"

On hearing this, David went purple with rage and, with his four hundred men, he prepared to wipe out Nabal's household. But as fate would have it, one of the servants alerted Abigail of the transaction between Nabal and David and the looming danger to her family. She took bread, wine, meat and fruits with her servants and rode up to meet David. Immediately, she saw David, she alighted from her ass, bowed to the ground and fell at his feet pleading for his forgiveness. Her words calmed the anger of David.

She was a wise woman who knew how to use her mouth and words well. This is a lesson to everyone. Her lifestyle has proved that our words can melt the hardest of hearts and because of her soothing and gracious words, she delivered her household from an unnecessary destruction.

UNMERITED HEALING THROUGH FAITH-FILLED WORDS

In Matthew 15:21-28, we are told of a woman of Canaan who cried after Jesus seeking deliverance for her daughter. For some reasons, He ignored her completely at first, but she was persistent in her plea. When Jesus finally answered her, He said that He was not sent to her but to the lost sheep of the house of Israel. One would have thought that she would have been angry with Jesus at this point.

In our present day, if a stranger had cried to a man of God for healing and got that kind of response, I'm pretty sure that the social media would have been a powerful medium of rebuking that man. I guess she had every right to be angry and tell Him that he wasn't living up to His profession. She could have reminded Him of His words that God had anointed him to preach the gospel to the poor, to heal the broken-hearted, to preach deliverance to the captives, recovering of sight to the blind and to set at liberty the bruised. She could have branded Him a liar who wanted fame but who was not really as good as many had perceived Him to be.

However, the words that further came from her are humbling for us all. Her life is more challenging because she wasn't an Israelite; she did not even serve the God of Israel. Her response so surprised Jesus that He commended her faith and resilience. He commended her use of words, her positivity in spite of His reaction. Jesus answered her and said, **"O woman. Great is thy faith: be it unto thee even as thou wilt"** and her daughter was healed immediately.

That woman did not allow anything to distract her from getting the desire of her heart. Nobody, not even Jesus could make her give up. I don't know if it was a test from Jesus or otherwise, but her story should stir us up to consistently and constantly use our words positively. This decision should not be based on other people's reaction towards us; it should be based on our own convictions, knowing the power that resides in our tongue.

One thing you may have observed from the stories I have shared with you is that confessions often spring from the heart. Using your mouth positively does not just happen. The Bible affirms that what we confess emanates from the abundance of our thoughts (Matthew 12:34). This means that there is an inextricable connection between the content of heart and the confessions of your tongue. Let's proceed to see how this works!

CHAPTER SIX

THOUGHTS AND WORDS: THE CONNECTION

"Either make the tree good, and his fruit good; or else make the tree corrupt, and his fruit corrupt: for the tree is known by his fruit" - Matthew 12:33

There is a connection between what we think and what we say. Nobody can ever learn to successfully control his mouth unless and until he first learns to control his mind. It is easy to offer a quick advice on controlling your mouth but that would be "like pulling off the top of a weed—unless the root is dug up, the weed always comes back."

To further buttress this fact, Joyce Meyer showed the necessary connection between the mind and the mouth thus: "What if I told you that the source of most of your problems could be found within you— We must realize and understand the power carried by our thoughts and words. They're so powerful that they can bring either blessings or curses into our lives."

HOW DOES THE MIND WORKS?

What is the human mind? Although every human possesses a mind, understanding it is not as easy as it may appear. What further complicates the puzzle is the fact that the mind is an invisible entity, having no observable features for easy description. Nevertheless, exploring the nature of the human mind in relation to the words we speak will be our focus in this chapter.

The mind is that part of man that reasons, thinks, feels, wills, perceives, judges, etc. This reveals the enormous function of the human mind. Every normal human mind exhibits the above features. This suggests why an individual who loses his mind is as good as dead, because what actually makes him a living being is the functioning of his mind. That is why when an individual misbehaves or behaves unnaturally, the natural question is, "Are you out of your mind?" The mind, indeed, is the man.

The mind, therefore, can be regarded as the engine or production house of human actions. Being the part of man that thinks implies that it generates ideas that define the man. This also has to do with the mind's power of imagination. This is the creative power of the mind which brings into existence things that aren't there and provoke either positivity or negativity in man. Although invisible, the mind also gives humans focus. In other words, it is commonly regarded as the seat of human consciousness, but it entails more than just human consciousness.

The human mind could also be simply understood as thought; in which case, one could be said to be having "double mind" or "a change of mind." It is the part of man that weighs and differentiates between evil and good things. It sets the boundary between what should be done and what shouldn't; between what is acceptable and what's forbidden. The human attributes of love, hatred, fear, kindness, compassion, wickedness, etc. and the power of recollection emanate from the mind. The mind is the center of all human emotions.

The power of perception of the human mind is very crucial to every individual's attainment in life. Your perception places you at an advantage over others. This means there are things you may notice which others are ignorant of. This justifies the claim that what you see is what you possess. But seeing in this instance is not necessarily what your physical eyes see, but what you perceive through your mind's eyes. In other words, it refers to your power of insight. A deep insight equips you with a better understanding of life. This is another vital function of the mind in relation to the spoken word because it is your insight and understanding that inspires your words.

The mind is the preparatory ground for human actions. A battle won from the mind will only need to be complemented by action, which could be in form of the spoken word. Your thoughts and feelings are first processed in the mind before you act on them. The spoken word is a product of that process. The mind communicated, therefore, the mind understood since no one has access to another's mind.

WHAT DOES THE SCRIPTURE SAY ABOUT THE MIND?

In terms of usage or function, the mind is used

interchangeably with the heart in the Scriptures. This is largely because the heart is used to mean the entire innermost part of man, which also includes the mind. This means that both the heart and mind are fused in function, **"For as [a man] thinketh in his heart, so is he..."** (Proverbs 23:7). This passage shows that thinking—which is a function of the mind—takes place in the heart.

Furthermore, the heart is synonymous with the mind (Hebrews 8:10; 1Samuel 2:35). Conscience and thought which are activities of the mind are said to take place in the heart, proving that both are used interchangeably (Matthew 9:4; Romans 2:15; 1Samuel 24:5; Acts 2:37). Moses' reference to his mind in Numbers 16:28 also connote the heart; compare Isaiah 44:19. The mind is also implied in the expression, "set his mind to" (Exodus 7:23). Similarly, the two parts of Psalm 73 verse 21 express the same thing. Thus, it is clear that in the Scriptures, the heart and the mind are used interchangeably to mean the same thing—the mind.

TWO KINDS OF MIND

We understand from the scriptures that there are broadly two kinds of mind: the good mind and the evil mind. While talking to His disciples, Jesus says that it is from within the heart, in this case, the human mind, that **"evil thoughts, adulteries, fornications, murders, Thefts, covetousness, wickedness, deceit, lasciviousness, an evil eye, blasphemy, pride, foolishness" proceed from "and defile the man"** (Mark 7:21-23).

It can be deduced, therefore, that the mind is a house that harbors all sorts of evils. This is the natural human mind. The term "proceed" suggests that these evils in the heart do not just idly remain there but come forth and defile a man. By implication, it means that people don't just get defiled by what they think but by what they say with their mouth or express in actions. People manifest their thoughts through speaking them and then going on to practice them.

In contrast, the good mind harbors good things for, **"A good man out of the good treasures of his [mind] bringeth forth that which is good"** (Luke 6:45). This then means that both good and evil words and actions proceed from the mind depending on the state of the mind in question. In other words, as a fountain sends forth streams, so does the mind send forth thoughts and expressions. The mind can be a fountain of good or evil depending on how clean or dirty the mind is.

THE MIND AND THE SPOKEN WORD

Recall that we have already established that the mind reasons, thinks, perceives and feels, and that our thoughts, feelings and perceptions are what we naturally express in our words. Herein lies the relationship between the mind and the spoken word.

Language is the instrument through which our mind is expressed. The spoken word is simply a product of the mind. The mind is the initiator of what every normal human being utters. In other words, your spoken words are like a show glass on which your mind is displayed. What you think (in your mind) is what you say and your utterance reveals the kind of person you are.

Jesus' lamentation in Matthew 12:34-37 over this generation is quite instructive in considering the human heart in relation to the spoken words:

O generation of vipers, how can ye, being evil, speak good things? for out of the abundance of the heart the mouth speaketh...But I say unto you, That every idle word that men shall speak, they shall give account thereof in the day of judgment. For by thy words thou shalt be justified, and by thy words thou shalt be condemned.

First, it is here revealed that the content of your speech would normally correspond with the state of your mind. If what is in your mind is negative (evil), the words you speak will be negative and subsequently yield unfavourable consequences. The reason is that your heart gives out from the abundance of its content. You naturally speak whatever has filled your mind, whether good or bad. While you may pretend so as to conceal your personality in your spoken words, you won't be able to do that always. For out of the abundance of the content of the heart, the mouth definitely must speak.

On a positive note however, Christ's observation also shows that the mind has the capacity to conceive great ideas. This is why you need to apply your mind to positive thinking that will give birth to positive utterances. It still needs to be reiterated that a man is what he thinks and says. Your thought as an element of your mind is a catalyst for change. Good thoughts applied in the right proportion and direction provokes positive action.

LIBERATION OR LIMITATION?

Your thought will either liberate or limit you in life. If you think you are not capable of accomplishing a particular task, then it's a pity because that task may never be accomplished. If you think you can't, then you surely can't, because the greatest motivation comes from within. What you will ever do and what you will ever be will more easily be achieved if you can picture it in your mind. Picture what you want to do, who you want to be, where you want to be, and their possibilities in your mind.

Your thought is like a seed planted and nurtured to maturity. If you allow the seed of the thought of failure in your mind, you will be surprised how it will grow and gradually come to reality. But you will be astounded that there are others in your shoes who were able to weather the storm and achieve great feats. The same situation where some people failed is where others were celebrated because of the difference in their mindsets.

What marked the end of the suffering of the prodigal son in Luke Gospel was the realization of his pathetic condition: **"He came to himself…"** (Luke 15:17). It wasn't that there was no solution to his seeming predicament but he never thought of it. Imagine how such a promising young man was wasting away in a foreign country when his father was such a wealthy and influential man. Is it that there is just no solution to that difficulty you are currently experiencing? Is there no greater height you can attain?

Thank God the prodigal son didn't stop at that realization but took a step further by rising up and going to meet his father, who was eagerly waiting for an opportunity to welcome him back home. That was a decisive step. It all begins in your mind. You may not need to relocate like the prodigal son, but having discovered you can achieve the utmost in life with a positive mindset, you need to apply the words of your mouth to change things in and around your life.

WHY DO PEOPLE HAVE NEGATIVE MINDS?

It is practically impossible for the natural man to think right. From the Fall of Man, his heart has always only been evil (Jeremiah 7:9). He may occasionally do or say the right things, but the constant and consistent reality is that his mind is in a corrupt state and thus, could only produce negative fruits. So, sin is the primary root cause of a negative and ungodly mind. And to be free from sin, you need to admit your helplessness to God and invite Christ Jesus to be the Lord of your life. He will cleanse you with His blood and make you a new creature from within.

However, aside from the problem of sin, there are some people who are naturally pessimistic; they hardly see anything positive about life. They are always too critical and expect nothing good from any situation. For such people, a negative mindset is inevitable. Also, ugly experiences in life make some people so hopeless that they don't believe there could still be anything good in life. Because of what they've been through, they don't see any cause to be hopeful. Life, to them, is meaningless.

Such people might have been disappointment or heartbroken and this suddenly made them become hardened at heart such that they no longer expect anything positive from life. Still, as it is with the problem of sin, there is good news for such people. If they can turn to Jesus and turn over their heartache and frustrations to Him, He will heal their broken hearts and bring consolations to their soul.

PROTECTING YOUR MIND

Seeing that your mind plays an enormous role on what you say and what eventually you become, wouldn't it be right to protect it? Of course, you'll agree that there is a need to jealously guard the fountain from which the words flow. An unguarded mind can ruin one's life. While it is good to watch one's utterances, it is safer to sanitize the very source of our utterances since only a good tree will naturally bear good fruits.

Many people have struggled to say positive things, but they are often amazed at their inability to control their utterances. Not that they are not aware of the danger of negative words but they are incapacitated. They simply can't help because the source is corrupt. The mind needs help. A good mind begets life changing utterances.

The writer of the Book of Proverbs instructs us to **"Keep thy heart with all diligence; for out of it are the issues of life"** (4:23). This instruction underscores the pivotal role of the heart and the imperative of protecting it from negative influences. The mind must be kept with all diligence, all seriousness and not with levity, because of the role it plays in making the man. The mind must be diligently kept because out of it are the actions of life. It is the wellspring of life; the source of life. If the mind is good, it will bring healing and health; but if it is contaminated, it will bring defilement and destruction.

Clearly, a good (transformed) mind is only guaranteed in God. Only God can give you a new mind because, until the mind is renewed or transformed into its former state before the fall, it can't consistently think right. Until a man begins a relationship with God, a sound mind is impossible. You can begin that today. Simply acknowledge that you are a sinner, confess you sins to God and forsake them. God will give you more grace to guard your mouth when you surrender your mind to Him.

More so, **"The heart of the wise teacheth his mouth, and addeth learning to his lips"** (Proverbs 16:23). Put in another way, those who know the power of words will let their heart (mind) instruct their mouth on what to say. Let your mind exercise control over your mouth. Don't be rash in talking. Think before you utter a word. Keep your heart against undue influence. Be mindful of what enters your heart. Be very mindful of what you nurse in your mind. You may not be able to stop negative thoughts from coming into your mind, but you can actually stop them from festering. Different negative thoughts may pervade your heart like evil eggs, but never let such eggs hatch in your heart. Resist them immediately and never allow them to stay. Avoid every form of contamination and corruption of your heart.

Aside from just guarding your mind against evil influence, as a Christian, it is expedient that you feed your mind with the nourishing diet of God's words. Just like the natural body, what you feed your mind determines the condition of your mind as a Christian.

Your mind will flourish if you constantly feed on God's infallible word. A mind saturated with the word of God doesn't lack uplifting and positive declaration. Such a mind is acquainted with the promises of God such that no situation escapes the sword of God's word issuing from your lips. The revelation we receive from God's word gives us live. By nature, the word of God is pure and it purifies and renews the mind, and by extension influences your utterances. It develops the mind in divine wisdom. And you will agree that the words of a man of wisdom doesn't only influence his life positively but liberate others around him.

When you equip your mind with the living word of God, you will speak life into situations. Challenges will bow at the proclamation of God's word. A mind inspired by the wisdom of God will be able to take a profitable decision in life as well. Even the devil himself couldn't withstand the cutting blade of God's words that issued from the Lord Jesus during His temptation (Matthew 4). So, study the word of God through every available means and your heart be properly nourished and your mouth won't lack the appropriate word at the right time for every situation.

Moreover, the human mind can also be positively influenced by listening to and reading good motivational speeches and books respectively. These have the effect of inspiring people towards being their best and actualizing their dreams. Some people are put down in their minds, sometimes because of ugly experiences. Such people may only need to be stirred. They need to wake the giant which circumstances have put down in their lives. A little relevant encouragement has refocused so many people. It inspires their minds with insights previously hidden to them. That is, it electrifies their dark state of mind.

Also, keeping a good company helps some people overcome their negative minds. If evil communication, according to the Scriptures, corrupts good manners (1 Corinthians 15:33), it invariably implies that good communication inspires good manner and speech, of course. A popular adage says, "Show me your friend and I will tell you who you are." This further buttresses the fact that people of good character will impart your life positively. Guard you heart and choose your friends wisely – then your words will reflect life and bring greatness into your destiny!

CHAPTER SEVEN

CONFESSING GOD'S WORDS

She held her only son in her arms, rocking him and willing his headache to go away. She whispered comforting words into his ears and was relieved to see that he had stopped moaning. Looking at his face, it seemed he had fallen asleep. But something felt strange. The hairs on her arms stood as she suddenly shivered as the hot afternoon breeze patted her skin. Fear gripped her heart. She took a long fearful look at her son again, observing him more closely. No rising and falling of the chest; she checked for a heartbeat—none. She checked for a pulse: nothing! A frightening scream threatened to escape her throat but she swallowed it. She took in a sharp breath and her breathing became heavy.

She refused to believe her eyes. No! Her son couldn't be dead. She gathered her son in her hands and headed straight to the room – the most sacred room in the house. She laid him on the bed – the one used by the man of God whenever he visited. She stood for a moment, watching for any sign of life from her son but he didn't stir. She left the room, locked the door and went in search of the man of God.

As she sought permission from her husband, he wondered why she wanted to see the man of God before the usual time. She stared at him for a moment, deciding whether to tell him or not, then she said, "It shall be well." Not sure of what to make of her behavior, her husband acceded to her request and off she went.

As she approached the house of the man of God, Elisha noticed her from afar and sent his servant to find out if everything was alright. All she said was "it is well!" Eventually, she poured out her grief and Elisha was compelled to go back with her.

This Shunammite woman had her dead son raised back to life and it was indeed well with her (2 kings 4). Why? Because, in the face of a colossal tragedy, she didn't use her mouth negatively. She confessed positively and her confession became her possession.

YOU WILL HAVE WHAT YOU SAY

Just as I highlighted in the previous chapter, not many people know the power in their mouth. Sadly, many Christians are in this category. They don't realize that the words they speak carry explosive dynamites that cause physical manifestation in their life. Let me remind you right now that every single word you speak is a seed that will germinate and bring forth multiple fruits in due time. Life and death are in the power of the tongue. You are what you say you are. If you say you are healed, you are healed. If you say that you will flourish like a palm tree, you will flourish. On the other hand, if you say you are doomed, you will be doomed. The Shunammite woman understood this fact, she used it appropriately and she got the result she wanted.

Positive confession is not just saying meaningless nice words; it is not avoiding realities neither is it denying the facts. It is a declaration of great possibilities in Christ Jesus. It is expressing faith in what God can do: calling those things that are not as though they were. Putting it in another way, "Positive confession is the practice of saying aloud what you want to happen with the expectation that God will make it a reality. To confess positively is to speak words that we believe or want to believe. This is opposed to negative confession which acknowledges hardship, poverty, illness and thus accepts them, refusing the ease, wealth and health God has planned for us."

Positive confession is not an act of talking God into doing that he doesn't want to do, it is confessing God's word in to that situation you have found yourself. If you are sick for instance and you say by His stripes I am healed (Isaiah 53:5), you expressing confidence in the finished work of Christ.

THE POWER OF CONFESSING GOD'S WORD

Positive confession increases your faith. According to Kenneth E. Haggin, confessing is affirming something we believe. Confession of God's words builds faith and faith confession creates reality. When your faith is built up, fear, worry and depression are dispelled. If you want to increase in faith, then take time to read God's word and confess what God has said about you or about that situation then you will experience a real breakthrough.

The fact is this, your confession determines your level of faith. It has the capacity to boost your faith into something more solid. When this happens you'll have this confidence to face any challenge life might throw your way.

Those who confess the word of God in whatever situation they find themselves tend to have a relaxed mind (as against being anxious and worried). They are optimistic and research has revealed that being optimistic improves your health tremendously.

Many years ago, a pastor was diagnosed with cancer. His church members who understood the power of confessing God's word encouraged him to select some verses on healing and read them to himself several times a day and every day. He obeyed and God healed him of that sickness. Confession of faith-filled words can release God's power to whatever situation you might have found yourself.

Someone said, "The words of Jesus in your mouth are still His words, therefore, they are spirit and life." Is there any area of your life that seems dead? Speak the Word of our Savior to it and life will be restored therein. God's word has an immense, unlimited power. It should be the basis for every confession you make. Read it. Store it up in your heart. Confess it and obey it and you will not only become an all-round conqueror but also an unstoppable force. The Scriptures confirm this when it states that the word of God should constantly be in the mouth of the Christian. He should meditate and think on it both in the day and in the night, observing to obey all that is written therein. For it is in doing this that prosperity and "good success" come (Joshua 1:8).

THE PRACTICE OF POSITIVE CONFESSION

Positive confessions improve your relationship. Positive confessions can lift your spirit and that of those around you. Just so you know, nobody likes to stay around hate speakers or negative people. What makes them negative? It may not be their actions but because of the negative things they enjoy saying.

Positive words can be a balm for a broken heart: they are just like honey, sweet to the soul, and health for the body (Proverb 16:24). Who wouldn't stay around a person whose words are sweet like honey? So before you open your mouth to say anything, don't forget that those words impact or weigh heavily on not only on you but also on those around you.

Positive confession increases your joy for "A man hath joy by the answer of his mouth: and a word spoken in due season, how good is it" (Proverb 15:23). Joyce Meyers once commented on Christian Post that

"Our joy is connected to what we say. And one of the ways we can instantly increase our joy is to stop talking about all of our problems." Even Apostle Peter through the inspiration of the Holy Spirit advised that if you really want to enjoy your life and see good days, refrain your tongue from negativity (1 Peter 3:10). So speak positively.

Your confessions can build faith and confidence in others. You can decide that henceforth, whatever comes out of your mouth must edify and minister grace to others. Eli, in 1 Samuel 1, realized that he had misjudged Hannah; so to make up, he decided to encourage her and assure her that God was going to grant her petition (1 Samuel 1:17). The effect of Eli's words on Hannah was that she brightened up, put herself together and even ate—something she had refused to do before.

Confessing positively encourages God to bless you. You should know that He is interested in blessing you and when you enthusiastically confess this, it depicts trust. Talking about childlike trust, have you ever watched the way children talk or rather brag about what their parents will do for them? Such attitude motivates the parent to go all out to get it done. This is what God expects from His children too. Your confidence in what He can do should reflect in your confessions.

IS THIS SCRIPTURAL?

Positive confession? Is it scriptural? It would interest you to know that some persons have argued that positive confession is not biblical. They claim that it is dangerous to believe that words have some mystical powers that help you get whatever you want. They also insist that it is a borrowed practice from some new-age concept and from Hinduism, where they teach a concept very similar to what is being discussed in this chapter. But this is a misrepresentation and a misinterpretation of the subject.

For the sake of clarity, you will recall that in chapter two, I talked about how God created the whole world using His words, and this same God created man in His own image. This means that man has a deposit of God within him. And when we talk about man being created in God's image, we are not talking about any physical features; we are talking about the ability to discern, relate, create, communicate and so on. And one of the precious gifts God has given to man, that sets him apart from other creatures, is the ability to use words. And by these words **"thou shalt be justified, and by thy words thou shalt be condemned"** (Matthew 12:37). So wouldn't you rather use your words positively, regardless of what other people or religions think or do about it?

Do you know that God actually expects you to confess positive things about your situation; because doing so is an indication that you trust God to come through for you? You'll recall the episode of the twelve spies sent to inspect the city of Canaan. More than anything else, this story reveals that God actually expects His children to confess faith and positivity in any given situation. Now it should be noted that the ten spies who gave the frightening reports did not lie about what they saw, they only stated the facts and that triggered a spiral of reactions from the children of Israel.

Numbers 14 clearly captured these reactions. If you read in Numbers 14:1-5, you'll picture how they went from self-pity to murmuring, regret, doubts and finally to rebellion. God couldn't have been more displeased. In Numbers 14:28, He pronounced his verdict. **"As truly as I live, saith the LORD, as ye have spoken in mine ears, so will I do to you."**

What have you been speaking into God's ears? Imagine, for a moment, that the children of Israel had reacted differently. What if they had declared God's faithfulness and ability to deliver like the three Hebrew children who said: **"Our God whom we serve is able to deliver us from the burning fiery furnace, and he will deliver us out of thine hand, O king"** (Daniel 3:17). This is positive confession and it is scriptural. So be careful with the things you say because what you say is what you get.

Confessing positively is the key to living a meaningful life on earth. The devil's primary mission is to steal, kill and destroy (John 10:10). He fights tooth and nail to get this done in the life of everyone. He brings discouraging moments, loss, fear, sorrow, sickness, death and despair to shatter us. However, the power to overcome every battle lies in the awesome power of our confessions. The scripture tells us that we will have whatever we say. That is why you cannot afford to always utter words of defeat and failure. Suffice it to say that you are your own prophet and you have to cultivate the habit of always confessing what God and the scriptures say about you.

Confessing positively cuts across every sphere of our life's endeavour. We can speak wholesome words concerning our children, our job, our spouses, our nation, our leaders, our churches, our relatives, our health, our finances and everything we can ever imagine. Whenever you confess what God or the scriptures hasn't spoken concerning you, you give the devil unlimited access to accomplish his evil plans in your life. It is high time you rose up and speak words of life and health.

Somebody reading this might be saying that confessing positively when one's world is breaking apart amounts to telling a lie. But I want you to know that confessing what God says about you amounts to believing in the name and power of Jesus. Jesus said emphatically that without faith, it is impossible to please God (Hebrews 11:6). So the next time you face a daunting situation and you confess negatively, you are not pleasing God. And when your life doesn't please God, it will definitely please the devil. I'm sure you do not want to spend the rest of your life pleasing the enemy of your soul.

STRIKING A BALANCE

At this juncture, it is important to state that, the world being what it is, many have come to understand the power of positive confession but they try to propagate it as a means of getting whatever they want. Some preachers encourage their adherents to speak themselves into wealth. They call it self-talk, positive assertions, power words and what have you. Seeing this, some Christians try to detach themselves from this practice and totally jettison positive confession. This is not so clever.

As children of God, we have been given the power to decree a thing and it will be established. With our words, we bring every contrary thought into captivity, into the obedience of Christ. Are you seriously going to give all that up because of people who twist the word of God to their own benefits? I think not. Acceding to this, Tom Brown said "Well, I refuse to surrender the truths of the Bible to the charlatans. Just because some false leader teaches biblical truths in a twisted manner does not mean that biblical truths are to be abandoned. This is what many Christians have done. They have handed over biblical truths to the devil's counterfeiters. This is just as foolish to do as it would be for the United States to quit making money because counterfeiters do the same."

Another aspect to consider is the fact that we don't always get what we say, no matter how intense or how often we say them. Put simply, some things don't actually come our way because we confess them. This is because of the fall of man at the beginning. Someone said our words have lost the power they had when Adam sinned and died spiritually. But this power can be regained when you're spiritually born anew, that is, when you are born again. At this point, you're made anew and the life of Christ comes into you. Although your words still may not have a strong hold but as you grow by feeding on God' word, your faith in God and His words increases. You abide in His word and you're saturated in it to the point that

His words become your words, then you will begin to experience the true power of positive confession.

This power is revealed when you come to the realization that it is not your carnal confession that brings about a manifestation, but rather, it is the confession of God's words, His testimonies and His promises. Again Tom Brown has an interesting perspective to this. "I am often asked by paranoid cult-watchers, "Do you believe in positive confession? I answer them, "No! I believe in the positive confession OF GOD'S WORD!" You see, it is not simply "positive confession" that is powerful.

It is the confession of "God's Word" that is powerful! I don't believe in speaking just anything and think that it is going to come to pass. No, I believe in speaking God's Word. God's Word is what is powerful, not my word. Someone might say, "If I confessed that I was going to be a millionaire, do you think I'm going to be one?" First of all, why do you confess that you are going to be a millionaire? "Because I want to be one." Fine, but where in the Bible does God promise to make you a millionaire? Nowhere does it promise you that. God does not promise to make you a millionaire, so don't bother to confess it, unless, of course, God gave you a special revelation that He wanted you to become a millionaire. In that case, it would be alright.

But, if God hasn't given you that revelation, then simply speak what He has promised you. He has promised to "supply all your needs according to His riches in glory by Christ Jesus." So put that promise in your mouth. Confess, "My God shall supply all my needs according to God's riches in glory by Christ Jesus." Now you are confessing God's Word. That Word is imperishable and incorruptible. However, saying that you are going to be a millionaire is like planting perishable seed—most likely it will not come to pass."

SILENCE YOUR GOLIATH WITH YOUR CONFESSION

Talking of making confessions based on God's word, His promises and testimonies, the story of David easily comes to mind. The Philistines had challenged the Israelites to a fight, and they produced their best warrior who happened to be a giant. David could not bear to see a Philistine rubbish the army of God. So, he sought King Saul's approval to fight Goliath. Saul tried to dissuade him but listen to David's testimony and you will understand what it means to make positive confession on the basis of God's promises:

"And Saul said to David, Thou art not able to go

against this Philistine to fight with him: for thou art but a youth, and he a man of war from his youth. And David said unto Saul, Thy servant kept his father's sheep, and there came a lion, and a bear, and took a lamb out of the flock: And I went out after him, and smote him, and delivered it out of his mouth: and when he arose against me, I caught him by his beard, and smote him, and slew him. Thy servant slew both the lion and the bear: and this uncircumcised Philistine shall be as one of them, seeing he hath defied the armies of the living God. David said moreover, The LORD that delivered me out of the paw of the lion, and out of the paw of the bear, he will deliver"** (1 Samuel 17:33-37). We all know how it ended: David conquered Goliath.

As a child of God, fill your mind with the word of God, speak it to yourself, speak it over your family, over your situation and your will experience victory. Speak it to the enemy and he will flee from you. Like the Shunammite woman, you too can make these confessions of faith: "it is well with my spirit", "it is well with my body", "it is well with my business" it is well with my finances", "it is well with my children", "it is well with our country", "it is well with our loved ones", "it is well with my soul." The word of God increases your faith.

Let me conclude this chapter by drawing your attention to a man who went through a great suffering and trauma. His wife, who should be strong for him and encourage him to see the light at the end of the tunnel, tried to persuade him to throw in the towel, curse God and die. This man, though in anguish and great pain still had the grace to make a positive confession. At one time he said, **"Though he slay me, yet will I trust in him"** At another time, he assured himself saying, I know my redeemer lives and regardless of what happens I will see God in my situation. You know what happened at the end? God gave him a double portion of all he had lost and multiplied his life. (See Job13:15; 19:25-26). What if he had thrown in the towel and cursed God? What if all he did during his trials was to dwell on his problems and confess negatively? It is certain that his story wouldn't have ended the way it did because he would have disappointed God.

There's something ironic about the confessions we make. Do you know that it takes more energy to speak negatively than it is to speak positively? So, understand that when you deliberately choose to shun negative thoughts and confessions and do the opposite, you are actually saving your energy for more useful undertakings. Research has also revealed that your appearance seems to improve or glow when confessing positive things. Try it out, watch out when a person is saying something positive, you'll find that they tend to look better.

MAINTAINING A HABIT OF POSITIVE CONFESSION

The world we live in is so filled with all manner of negativities, as such, it may not be easy to always confess positively but with these suggestions below, you should be able to cultivate the habit of making positive confessions:

- Fill your mind with the word of God. Meditate on it and daily confess it over every situation.

- Stop meditating on your problems and all the negativities around.

- Make a deliberate decision to say positive things.

- Look for something positive even in the midst of negativities. For instance, if everyone seems to be talking about economic recession, you can decide to say, "Oh thank goodness, our God can never go bankrupt, and we are His children. This will automatically lift everyone's spirit."

- Avoid negative people. Negative attitude can be

contagious.

- Think positive thoughts, because our words are just expressions of our thoughts.

- Practice regularly. Someone once said positive confession is a skill. It can only become a part of you when you do it regularly.

CHAPTER EIGHT

THE POWER OF "I CAN"

I said it earlier that the reason many people speak negatively about themselves is because they have a wrong mindset. Negative thinking and a wrong perception have been largely responsible for the failure and low living of many people. They never see themselves as succeeding beyond their present state. They call themselves a failure even before they try their hands on anything and they actually fail when they eventually try. The reason isn't because they were meant to fail, but because they think they were going to fail.

The truth of the matter is that you're the active force of your life. It is you who decides whether you succeed or fail, no other person. Not even the devil; it's you.

If you failed, then you caused it and if you succeeded, it's also because you also caused it.

Someone has rightly stated that "you can succeed if nobody believes in you, but you can't succeed if you don't believe in yourself." No one can deny the fact that self-belief is a very important factor in success. The reason you are where you are is due largely to what you have believed. If you believe you're small, then you are. But if you believe you're great, then you're on your way there.

You can't achieve great things if you think small of yourself. No one who ever became great did so by thinking small of himself. This kind of mindset will keep you stuck for the rest of your life. It will hinder you from moving forward. Self-doubt, lack of self-confidence and fear are three reasons why people fail to move forward in life. The doubt they have for themselves and the fear of the unknown chain them to their present uncomfortable state. Until you break out of such self-imposed prison, you can never move forward.

In his book, Light Up Your World, Charles Ayidu tells a popular story about an eagle, which died without fulfilling its potentials as an eagle just because of what it believed of itself. As the story goes, a mother eagle had laid her eggs in her nest which was located on the edge of a mountain. One fateful day, an earthquake rocked the mountain, causing one of the eggs to roll down the mountain into a chicken farm, mingling with the eggs of the chickens in the farm. Not knowing what had happened, one of the chickens brooded over the eagle's egg, thinking it was one of hers.

In the course of time, the egg hatched and out came a beautiful eaglet. But since he was being raised by chickens and he lived amongst them, it wasn't long before the eagle began to believe he was just another chicken. As the days passed, sometimes the eagle would look up and admire the eagles soaring up high in the skies, and then he would cry, "Oh, I wish I could soar like those birds." The chickens around would then burst out laughing at what they thought was a ridiculous wish by the eagle. They would then go ahead to say something like, "Oh, sorry. You cannot soar like those birds, because you are a chicken, and chickens don't fly."

As the eagle grew older, he continued to stare up at what was his real family, dreaming and wishing that he could be like them. Anytime he made his wishes known to the chickens, they always told him he couldn't fly. Eventually, the eagle came to believe what the chickens had always told him—that he was a chicken, and so, he couldn't fly. Soon, the eagle ceased dreaming and all his desire to fly evaporated, and he continued to live his life like every other chicken.

Finally, after living a long life as a chicken, the eagle passed away. He neither knew the purpose for which he was born nor did he fulfill his potentials as an eagle. He never for once experienced the delight of flying above the clouds and scaling the topmost mountains. Instead of growing into the king of birds, he only ate worms and made his bed in the dust.

But why did the eagle die unfulfilled? Why did he die with all his potentials? The answer is simple: he only saw himself as just another chicken. There was no way he was going to go higher than what he thought of himself. It's up to you to decide whether you want to soar like the eagle or you want to die like the chicken.

BELIEVE IN YOURSELF

The question is how do you see yourself? What do you think of yourself? What do you believe about yourself? Do you believe you can? Do you believe you're greater than what you are at present? Do you believe that there are still far greater heights you can still get to? Yes, you can, if you believe and work towards it. Yes! You can be anything you want to be if you believe you can and you run towards the goal.

You were created for something big. It doesn't matter what your present situation is, you weren't created a failure. You have the capacity and ability to do great things and bless your generation. Don't be afraid of launching out and doing what's in your mind to do simply because you're afraid of what people might think or because you're afraid you might fail. Failure isn't final. It's an opportunity to learn and begin again more brightly. You're not inadequate, you're not disabled, and you're not a failure!

If I may ask you, what are you afraid of? What's keeping you down from rising above the shadows? The only thing keeping you from becoming who you were created to be is yourself. Marianne Williamson was right when she said, "our deepest fear is not that we are inadequate. Our deepest fear is that we are powerful beyond measure. It is our light, not our darkness, that most frightens us."

Yes, you're powerful beyond measure. You're powerful beyond what you think. She further asked, "We ask ourselves, 'Who am I to be brilliant, gorgeous, talented, fabulous?' Actually, who are you not to be?" Is there any reason you can't be or shouldn't be? Weren't you created by God? Didn't He create you in His image?

Hasn't He deposited in you everything that you need to be what He created you for? Believe in yourself friend! There isn't any limitation to what you can achieve if you believe in yourself and in what God has deposited in your life.

Have faith in your abilities. You do yourself and the world no good by thinking small of yourself or by withdrawing from what you should do. It's not humility. It's inferiority complex. Those who allow this complex to control their life and define their existence are the most pathetic people in the world. I say again, believe in yourself, friend! The apostle Paul said, **"I can do all things through Christ which strengtheneth me"** (Philippians 4:13). Repeat those words until they sink into you.

Believe what God has revealed about you in the Bible. Faith in the promises of God will build your self-confidence and transform your language. Read the word of God and meditate on it and it will fill you with faith, which will build you up for great confessions and possessions in life; for **"faith cometh by hearing, and hearing by the word of God"** (Romans 10:17).

Did you know what Jesus said about those who had faith and believed? In Matthew 17:20 He said to His disciples, **"If ye have faith . . . nothing shall be impossible unto you."** Did you see that? Nothing shall be impossible to you if you will believe that it is possible.

By the word of God, build your self-esteem in God. As a child of God, the thought that God is with you should fill you with hope and confidence. He is with you and through you, He has promised to do great and mighty things on the earth. Doesn't that produce a great feeling? Of course, it does!

Therefore, stop thinking small; think and dream big. Achieving great things in life begins with a single thought. A single thought that grows until it takes over the whole being of the individual. It consumes his psychology and mixes with his emotions until it becomes the only thing he is living for. This is the kind of dream that takes a man to the top. So, if you want to achieve something significant in life, then begin to dream big.

Be positive. Trust in your dream and ideas. Believe it's possible If you don't trust your dream, then don't expect anybody to do either. To believe consistently that it's possible for you to achieve anything you put your mind into and that it's possible for you to win in any situation you find yourself is to cultivate the winning mentality. Having the right attitude will help you overcome any situation. Karl Menninger says, "Attitudes are more important than facts" and that's spot on. Your attitude and reaction to situations will always determine whether you'll overcome or be defeated.

PURSUE YOU DREAM

Those who believe they can achieve their dreams and rise above any obstacle don't just sit down and do nothing. They don't just dream and end there; they pursue their dreams. They put action to intention. It's not enough to just dream and believe, you need to go after your dream.

Someone once said that nothing can be achieved in the abstract. You can't achieve something out of nothing; you must first create the reality in your mind and then pursue it. Nothing ventured, nothing gained. According to Pastor Sunday Adelaja, "the future will bring a breakthrough to those who not only make a decision today but also begin to take certain steps toward what they have planned. This is the law of getting results." It's not enough to have a dream, it's important to know how to accomplish the dream.

How do you pursue your dream? In pursuing your dream, you must make adequate plan for it. As the saying goes, if you fail to plan, you plan to fail. Write it down and let it be clear. The Holy Bible advises us to

"Write the vision, and make it plain upon tables, that he may run that readeth it." (Habakkuk 2:2). It is said that the faintest pen is sharper than the sharpest brain. This is to say that whatever you don't put down, you easily forget as time wears on. Document your ideas, your strategies and the steps you want to take towards the actualization of that dream. Make it so clear that anyone who comes across you won't be left in doubt about what it is.

In addition, you should acquire skills or knowledge that relate to your dream. Everything you do and every activity you get involved in should have a direct or indirect relationship with your goal. It serves as a constant reminder of where you are going.

Get out of your comfort zone. Nothing good comes cheap, it comes at a price. It was Thomas Edison who said that "genius is 1 percent inspiration and 99 percent perspiration."

KEEP YOUR MIND ON IT

Many have derailed from their dream, not because they didn't believe they could achieve it, but because they lost their focus along the way. They couldn't keep their eyes on the goal to the end. To achieve your dream, you can't switch your mind off and on, your mind must stay on the goal; you can't take your feet off the pedal, or else you'll fall away. Focus is the power of concentration on a clear and specific object. The ability to keep your eye on your dream despite distractions.

There will be obstacles on your way, but you have to be determined to fulfill your dream. Anyone who ever achieved his dream has had to fight his way through obstacles. See the obstacles as stepping stones to success. Don't react negatively to any situation that crosses your path. Find the positive; find a way to turn it into your advantage. Staying focused till the end will take an insuperable drive, doggedness and sacrifice.

Stick to the plan and pursue it. Don't make an alternative in case you fail. This is a recipe for failure. It's either you succeed or you succeed, there is no other choice. Andres Lara says that "The commitment to make things work is only found where there is no alternative plan to fall back on; at this moment, plan A simply has to work because there's no other choice." And George Shults adds that "the minute you start talking about what you're going to do if you lose, you have already lost."

Napoleon Hill, in his book Think and Grow Rich, tells a story of a great warrior who went to war against a very powerful foe whose men outnumbered his. Knowing that it would take something extraordinary for him to come out victorious, he did something unusual. He loaded his soldiers into boats and sailed into the enemy's territory. When they arrived there, he gave the order to burn the ships that brought them. As the flames rose into the air, he addressed his men saying, "You see the boats going up in smoke. That means that we cannot leave these shores alive unless we win. We now have no choice—we win or perish." They won the war. That's the power of focus and rugged determination. You should put on such attitude.

Deliberately cut off from things that add no value to your pursuit and surround yourself with things that would constantly remind you of the goal ahead of you. Don't procrastinate. Procrastination has been rightly described as the thief of time. It gives you a job to do while it steals what's most important from you.

Yes, you can! Only believe! Just as Andres Lara puts it, "Nothing happens unless a firm belief precedes it. A firm belief is the foundation to every accomplishment. Sooner or later, those who succeed in life are not the ones with greater advantages, but those who firmly believe they can." Let me leave you with the words of Walter D. Wintle:

THE POWER OF YOUR WORD

If you think you are beaten you are;
If you think you dare not you, don't;

If you want to win but you think you can't;
It's almost a cinch you won't.
If you think you'll lose, you're lost.

For out of the world we find
Success begins with a fellow's will;
It's all in a state of mind.

Life's battles don't always go
To the stronger and faster people,
But sooner or later the people who win are the people who think they can.

I can. What do you think? Success only comes to those who believe they can and work towards it in faith. Let your life and words always reflect what you desire, and you'll soon find your desire becoming a glorious reality.

THE GREATEST PRAYER OF A LIFETIME

The greatest prayer of a lifetime is to be reconnected back to God in a living relationship. Relationship is the basis for asking. You cannot pray to a God whom you don't know and who does not know you. God wants to be intimate with you. This type of relationship is available to each one of us when we sincerely repent of our sins, ask for God's forgiveness, and receive His Son, Jesus, as our personal Lord and Savior. If you have never surrendered your life to God, or if you have turned away from God and you want to return to Him, now is the time. God is waiting for you. His arms are open wide to receive you. Just pray this simple prayer right now:

O Lord, be merciful to me, a sinner. I realize that I am a sinner. I need a Savior and you are my savior. I repent of every sin, every wrongdoing, and I ask for your forgiveness. I receive Jesus Christ, Your only begotten Son, as my Lord and my Savior. I believe that Jesus went to the cross for me and paid the price for my salvation, and now I receive Him into my heart. I declare that I am born again. I am a child of God. Old sins are gone, and I have a brand-new life in Christ in Jesus' name. Amen.

If you prayed this prayer and wish to contact Pastor Yemi for guidance, please email him at: info@yemioyinkansola.com

ABOUT PASTOR YEMI OYINKANSOLA

Pastor Yemi Oyinkansola, a professional banker called into full time ministry is a teacher and an encourager with deep spiritual insight.

He is a worshipper and a prayer warrior who believes that all things are possible through God when you engaged in intensive worship and fervent prayer through faith.

He Pastors with the Redeemed Christian Church of God in California USA where he resides with his beautiful wife Comfort and two lovely children, Melody and Toluwani.

www.ingramcontent.com/pod-product-compliance
Lightning Source LLC
Chambersburg PA
CBHW070647050426
42451CB00008B/307